Supporting Children with Fun Rules for Tricky Spellings

This illustrated workbook has been created to support learners who, after acquiring the basics of reading and writing, have struggled to organically grasp the rules that govern spelling in the English language. Each photocopiable worksheet is designed to support a key spelling rule, explored in the colourful storybook *Who Put the Spell into Spelling?* This activity workbook is designed to be used alongside the storybook.

Key features include:

- Twenty-two activity worksheets designed to help learners understand and practise key spelling rules
- Activities designed to support skills in reading, spelling and writing
- Quirky illustrations designed to make the rules come to life

Developed with feedback from teachers and students, this is an invaluable resource for teachers and parents looking to support learners who find spelling a challenge, or who are learning English as an additional language.

Georgie Cooney: I now live in Co Cork, Ireland with 'my family and other animals'. I grew up in North Yorkshire before being 'shipped off' to boarding school and then onto Durham University.

I started my career as a primary school teacher but very quickly learnt that my interest and skills lay in working with learners with difficulties. I think I am able to relate to those who, like me, 'think out of the box'.

I have taught in schools nationally and internationally. Before moving to Ireland, as well as teaching, I trained teachers and adults to work with learners with Specific Learning Difficulties (SpLDs). I gained so much from my students and I keep learning every day. I hope this book set helps you to learn too.

T0383381

Supporting Children with Fun Rules for Tricky Spellings: An Illustrated Workbook

Written by **Georgie Cooney**

Illustrated by **Molly Hickey**

Educational Consultant: **Christine Kelly**

Routledge
Taylor & Francis Group

LONDON AND NEW YORK

First published 2020
by Routledge
2 Park Square, Milton Park, Abingdon, Oxon OX14 4RN

and by Routledge
52 Vanderbilt Avenue, New York, NY 10017

Routledge is an imprint of the Taylor & Francis Group, an informa business

© 2020 Georgie Cooney

The right of Georgie Cooney to be identified as author of this work has been asserted by her in accordance with sections 77 and 78 of the Copyright, Designs and Patents Act 1988.

All rights reserved. The purchase of this copyright material confers the right on the purchasing institution to photocopy pages which bear the photocopy icon and copyright line at the bottom of the page. No other part of this publication may be reproduced, stored in a retrieval system, or transmitted in any form or by any means, electronic, mechanical, photocopying, recording or otherwise, without prior permission in writing from the publisher.

Trademark notice: Product or corporate names may be trademarks or registered trademarks, and are used only for identification and explanation without intent to infringe.

British Library Cataloguing-in-Publication Data
A catalogue record for this book is available from the British Library

Library of Congress Cataloging-in-Publication Data
A catalog record has been requested for this book

ISBN: 978-0-367-81962-0 (pbk)
ISBN: 978-1-003-01106-4 (ebk)
ISBN: 978-0-367-81960-6 (Set)
ISBN: 978-1-003-01104-0 (Set) (ebk)

Typeset in Avenir and VAG Rounded
by Servis Filmsetting Ltd, Stockport, Cheshire

Printed and bound by CPI Group (UK) Ltd, Croydon, CR0 4YY

Dedication

This is dedicated to Michael Thomas Aloysius Cooney, my adorable dad. His dyslexia meant that he found spellings a challenge in life. Nevertheless, he loved life and life loved him and he successfully made the most of it!

So this is also dedicated to all those people who find that they have to put extra effort into spelling words. It is VERY frustrating so I hope this Book Set helps you, even if it's just a little bit.

Love from a not-very-good speller,

Georgie

Contents

Acknowledgements

I originally wrote this book in 2006, a long time ago now. I knew then that it was something that could help learners to become better spellers, but I had to see it in practice.

Christine Kelly, a specialist teacher, was instrumental in implementing the lessons over the years and making them fun. More importantly for me, she was able to tell me exactly what worked and what didn't work. She challenged me on a number of occasions and this is exactly what I needed to ensure that this book could reach its objective: to store spelling rules in the learners' memories. She is a wonderful teacher and a brilliant advisor. Thank you Christine.

There were many illustrators who filled a variety of rubbish bins with their ideas and it all seemed a bit hopeless at one point. It was by chance that I saw some Christmas card pictures drawn by my cousin **Molly Hickey**. They were visually brilliant. It was then by good fortune that Molly had the amazing vision that she had. How does anyone bring an alphabet letter alive? Well, Molly managed it somehow with her fabulous and rare artistic skills and I can't thank her enough.

Joff Brown took a chance on us and shared the vision that we all had for this book. He completely understood what we were looking for and he just put his head down and got on with the task involved. He is clearly a talented and skilled editor.

My spelling guru and my mum, **Mary-Rose Cooney**. Thank you for being a wonderful sounding board and teacher of the English language. You are a skilled grammar and punctuation pioneer!

My husband **Aaron**. A dyslexic who wishes he had had this book when growing up. Thank you for using your amazing dyslexic brain to make this spelling book what it is.

Introduction

PLEASE DO READ THIS BEFORE STARTING THE WORKSHEETS – THIS IS REALLY IMPORTANT AND WON'T TAKE LONG TO READ.

Who Put the Spell into Spelling? has been devised to help learners memorise and use spelling rules that are tricky to remember. There are many spelling rules but the ones included here have been chosen because I think that these are the most important. We all know as adults that, unfortunately, our spellings are vital for first impressions. When others read our written words, they make judgements about us, whether we like it or not. This resource is to give all of us a better opportunity in life and to ensure that people get the right impression of us!

Why have I written this book?

I only discovered these rules later on in life. I learnt 'but a few' spelling rules when I was at school, so when I discovered the long list of them, I felt cheated. I wished that I had known these helpful spelling tips in the hope that I could speed up my writing and spell with more accuracy. On the plus side, this upset only led me to create this story.

I wanted to find a memorable way for learners to hold the information in their brain. It needed to be visual yet easy to talk about too. There needed to be connections and reasons for some of these rules. Surely it is at school where we first learn the importance of rules so I decided to have all the alphabet letters in school too!

Who are the storybook and workbook intended for?

The storybook is to be read and completed alongside the workbook. For non-independent learners, this could be done with a teacher, parent or a trusted adult. It is important to point out that this book has been written for those children or young people who have struggled to bridge the transition from learning to read and spell – to reading to learn to spell and write. I hope learners of any age beyond 7 or 8 years old will find the story engaging. The reason I suggest this age is because the learner is going to need some basic skills and knowledge first.

Ideally, before starting this book, they will already know the following:

Phonological awareness and phonics* (don't worry if you have never heard of these before, I hadn't either in the beginning days).

1. They will know what a syllable* is and be able to break up and blend syllables (speaking/listening)
2. They will be able to identify and produce rhyming* words (speaking/listening)
3. They will know that words can be split into phonemes* (letter sounds) and graphemes* are used to represent those phonemes, e.g. /ir/ in bird is represented with the letters 'i' and 'r'
4. They will know how to read and spell the alphabet letters in and out of the alphabet sequence
5. They will know how to read and spell phonics* or letter sounds (including digraphs*)

The importance of the letter sounds

It is so EXTREMELY important that the letter sounds are never enunciated with a schwa*. Children are taught to say short sounds rather than long sounds for many good reasons. There are lots of examples of these on the Internet, so please do search for examples of phonic sounds if you're not confident with this. We use around 44 sounds in the English language so there is a lot of learning going on, whilst also trying to read and spell!

Being prepared

If the learner is not confident with the 5 stages of learning listed above, please ensure that they become stronger in these skills, ideally before you start working on *Who Put the Spell into Spelling?* Our aim is to strengthen strengths and weaken weaknesses. We don't want learners starting off feeling unarmed or lacking in basic skills.

Our memories and learning

There are so many reasons why we might find spelling hard. Depending on the learners' strengths and weaknesses, there could be an assortment of obstacles in the way.

To begin with, the relationship between speech sounds (phonology*) and spelling patterns (orthography*) is very wobbly and can't be trusted. As you read above, the *44 sounds* we have in English are challenging to learn.

When children learn to spell, they start to use their background knowledge to help them recognise patterns in spelling. Here are some examples:

- If they can identify and generate rhyme*, then it is more likely that they will see rimes* in word families and then have more success spelling them e.g. ill, fill, chill, spill, thrill, thrilling, killing etc.
- If they can divide and blend syllables then it is more likely that they will recognise that every syllable must have a vowel sound. This will help them to ensure that they will have more success spelling with syllable analysis e.g. 'cat-er-pill-ar'.
- If they can identify and build phonemes then it is more likely that they will have success spelling words by encoding using their phonic knowledge.

Why bother with this book when there is so much more to learn?

The reason for the need for this book is that in addition to all the skills for spelling listed above; you then have to learn a load of spelling rules! This is a unique resource, one of a kind and it is a necessity for many who have struggled with spelling thus far.

The science

It is well known that we use different parts of our brains for different functions.

Furthermore, every individual uses his or her brain differently. Our SpLD learners have many strengths and talents, which help them to compensate for their specific difficulties. These difficulties can be epitomised in:

- Sequencing
- Working memory
- Rapid naming
- Processing (often phonological)
- Acquiring literacy skills.

Producing written words is a complicated process involving different mechanisms in a variety of regions in the brain. I am hoping that by tapping into as many of these areas or senses as possible, we will eventually help learners to remember these tricky spelling rules. It should in turn help speed up the writing process too.

The worksheets

In order to ensure that we are helping our learners to store as much information in their brain as possible, we have created worksheets that make one use the following skills:

1. **<u>Reading</u>** – **decoding*** – recognising words accurately because of known patterns and spelling rules
2. **<u>Spelling</u>** – **encoding*** – spelling words accurately because of known patterns and spelling rules
3. **<u>Writing</u>** – using the motor skills to help implement what they have decoded and what they have encoded.

Note: If or when the exceptions to the rules arise, then don't be afraid of them.

Discuss them, play with them, have fun with them. You could even go and look for them. They do exist and they need to be known. The more multi-sensory the learning, the more likely it is that things will be remembered.

* For definitions of these words, please refer to the **Glossary** at the back of this workbook, p. 93.

Worksheet 1

How well do we know our letter names and sounds?

This involves you, as the adult, listening to activities 1 and 2 and then delivering names and sounds in activities 3 and 4. Make a note of any weaknesses and try to reinforce the teaching of these names and sounds throughout the story.

Adult: Letters have names and sounds. Let's see how well you know them.

1. Please say out loud the names of these letters in this order.

   (All of these should be names as we hear them in the alphabet.)

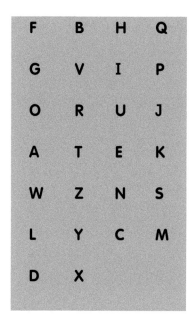

F	B	H	Q
G	V	I	P
O	R	U	J
A	T	E	K
W	Z	N	S
L	Y	C	M
D	X		

2. Now say out loud the sounds of these letters in this order.

   (These should be letters sounds without a schwa. They should be short sounds. See the words we have given you to help match the sound to the beginning sound in the word.)

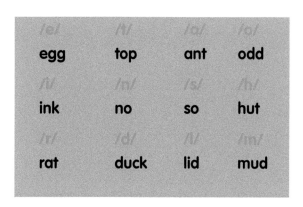

/e/	/t/	/a/	/o/
egg	top	ant	odd
/i/	/n/	/s/	/h/
ink	no	so	hut
/r/	/d/	/l/	/m/
rat	duck	lid	mud

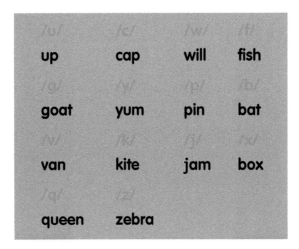

/u/	/c/	/w/	/f/
up	cap	will	fish
/g/	/y/	/p/	/b/
goat	yum	pin	bat
/v/	/k/	/j/	/x/
van	kite	jam	box
/q/	/z/		
queen	zebra		

3. Now spell the following letter names in the order that they are given.

    (You dictate these alphabet names in this order to the learner):

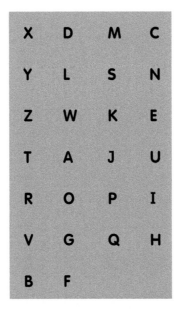

X	D	M	C
Y	L	S	N
Z	W	K	E
T	A	J	U
R	O	P	I
V	G	Q	H
B	F		

4. Now spell the following letter sounds in the order that they are given.

    (You dictate these sounds in the following order, saying the sound first, followed by an example of the words where the sound is heard).

    NB: The /x/ sounds like 'cks', which is why giving 'box' is the most helpful way of delivering the sound. It is also used in phonics schemes so the learners recognise it.

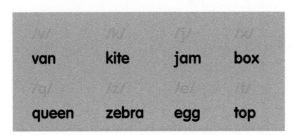

/v/	/k/	/j/	/x/
van	kite	jam	box
/q/	/z/	/e/	/t/
queen	zebra	egg	top

/a/	/o/	/i/	/n/
ant	odd	ink	no
/s/	/h/	/r/	/d/
so	hut	rat	duck
/l/	/m/	/u/	/c/
lid	mud	up	cap
/w/	/f/	/g/	/y/
will	fish	goat	yum
/p/	/b/		
pin	bat		

Worksheet 2

Rule 1: Magic E makes the other vowel sounds say their names

When **e** is put at the end of a word, it makes the single **vowel** in the word say its alphabet name e.g. hope. (Some people say the **short vowel** becomes a **long vowel**.) This is also known as split **e**, split **digraph**, silent **e**, mute **e**.

1. **Read out loud** the following words using **Magic E** for the words in the second column.

Words with vowel sounds	Words with vowel names – Magic E
cub	cube
cut	cute
mat	mate
sit	site
pet	Pete
pip	pipe
cap	cape

hop

hope

cod

code

2. **Spell** the following **Magic E** words using Rule 1 and the clues and pictures to help you.

If the learner is struggling to find the word, use 'hangman' to help you get the answer.

1. **Sixth month of the year:** _____.

JFMAMJJAS

2. **Something you can fly, high in the sky:** _____.

3. **A material used for building:** _____.

4. **Found on a lion:** _____.

5. **Helps you to smell:** _____.

3. **Rewrite** the following words into the correct order in the sentence. Add one of the missing **Magic E** words from activity 2 to complete each sentence.

1. playing rugby broke his he

   He _____ _____ _____ _____ rugby.

2. fly let's go and a

   Let's _____ _____ _____ _____ _____.

3. are a diamonds precious

   Diamonds _____ _____ _____ _____.

4. month my favourite summer is

   My _____ _____ _____ _____ _____.

5. lion roaring the rough had a

   The _____ _____ _____ _____ _____ _____.

Worksheet 2 Answer

Rule 1: Magic E makes the other vowel sounds say their names

Exercise 2

1. Sixth month of the year: June

2. Something you can fly, high in the sky: kite

3. A material used for building: stone

4. Found on a lion: mane

5. Helps you to smell: nose

Exercise 3

1. He broke his nose playing rugby.

2. Let's go and fly a kite.

3. Diamonds are a precious stone.

4. My favourite summer month is June.

5. The roaring lion had a rough mane.

Worksheet 3

Rule 2: V before E at the end of words

v comes before **e** at the end of a word ending with a /**v**/ sound. e.g. grave

1. **Read out loud** the following words:

Words ending with 've':

above	drove
nerve	solve
glove	alive
dove	captive
chive	creative
carve	serve
grave	behave
brave	leave
curve	relative
cave	active

2. **Spell** the following **'ve' words** using Rule 2 and the clues and pictures to help you.

If the learner is struggling to find the word, use 'hangman' to help you get the answer.

1. It is more than 'like' and uses the heart: _____.

2. A delicious bite to eat, can be green or black: _____.

3. An old-fashioned cooker, which gets very warm: _____.

4. You do this to remove hair: _____.

5. This is where someone is buried when they die: _____.

3. **Rewrite** the following words into the correct order in the sentence. Add one of the missing **'ve' words** from activity 2 to complete each sentence.

1. hair to remove can you

   You _____ _____ _____ _____ hair.

2. friends my I much very

   I _____ _____ _____ _____ much.

3. died when buried we in a it cat our

   When _____ _____ _____, _____ _____ _____ _____ _____ _____.

4. cook you porridge a on can

   You _____ _____ _____ _____ _____ _____.

5. colour green favourite my is

   _____ _____ _____ _____ _____ colour.

Worksheet 3 Answers

Rule 2: V before E at the end of words

Exercise 2

1. It is more than 'like' and uses the heart: love

2. A delicious bite to eat, can be green or black: olive

3. An old-fashioned cooker, which gets very warm: stove

4. You do this to remove hair: shave

5. This is where someone is buried when they die: grave

Exercise 3

1. You can shave to remove hair.

2. I love my friends very much.

3. When our cat died, we buried it in a grave.

4. You can cook porridge on a stove.

5. Olive green is my favourite colour.

Worksheet 4

**Rule 3: Y says the name of 'i' at the end
of words**

y can replace **i** at the end of words or **syllables** but still sounds like **i**'s name.
e.g. my or myself

1. **Read out loud** the following words:

'y' replaces 'i' at the end of words and says its name

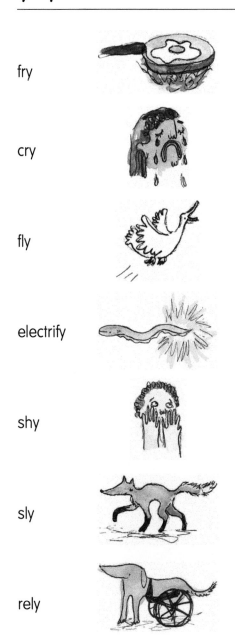

fry

cry

fly

electrify

shy

sly

rely

deny

retry

2. **Spell** the following **'y' words** using Rule 3 and the clues and pictures to help you.

If the learner is struggling to find the word, use 'hangman' to help you get the answer.

1. **The seventh month of the year:** _____. JFMAMJJASOND

2. **Another word for a secret agent:** _____.

3. **The opposite of wet:** _____.

4. **Where you can see clouds and stars:** _____.

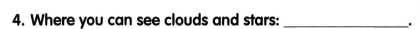

5. **Another word for 'answering someone':** _____.

3. **Rewrite** the following words into the correct order in the sentence. Add one of the missing **'y' words** from activity 2 to complete each sentence.

1. towel swimming I get to after use a

   I _____ ____ _____ _____ _____ _____ _____ swimming.

2. soon send will as possible him to I a as

   I _____ _____ ____ _____ ____ ____ ____ _____ ____ possible.

3. Russian in was he London living a

   He _____ _____ _____ _____ _____ _____ London.

4. is when begin ends the summer and school holidays

   _____ ___ _____ _____ _____ ____ ____ _____ _____ begin.

5. in high aeroplane I an saw up the

   I _____ ____ _____ _____ ____ ____ _____ _____.

Worksheet 4 Answers

Rule 3: Y says the name of 'i' at the end of words

Exercise 2

1. The seventh month of the year: July

2. Another word for a secret agent: spy

3. The opposite of wet: dry

4. Where you can see clouds and stars: sky

5. Another word for 'answer': reply

Exercise 3

1. I use a towel to get dry after swimming.

2. I will send a reply to him as soon as possible.

3. He was a Russian spy living in London.

4. July is when school ends and the summer holidays begin.

5. I saw an aeroplane high up in the sky.

Worksheet 5

Rule 4: Y says the name of 'e' at the end of words

y can replace '**e**' at the end of words but still sounds like **e**'s name.

e.g. angry (often seen in **adjectives**, **adverbs** and **nouns**)

1. **Read out loud** the following words:

---

y can replace and say 'e's name at the end of words.

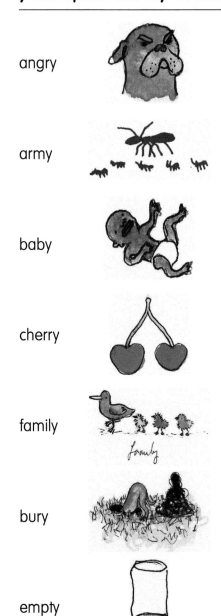

angry

army

baby

cherry

family

bury

empty

sorry

penalty

2. **Spell** the following **'y' words** using Rule 4 and the clues and pictures to help you.

If the learner is struggling to find the word, use 'hangman' to help you get the answer.

1. You might have to see a doctor if you get an _____.

2. When you haven't eaten enough food,

you can feel really _____.

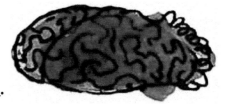

3. Sometimes it's really hard to store spellings

in your _____.

4. He was a gentleman and she was a _____.

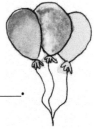

5. When we celebrate something, we can have a _____.

3. **Rewrite** the following words into the correct order in the sentence. Add one of the missing **'y' words** from activity 2 to complete each sentence.

1. old their sometimes people lose can

   Old _____ _____ _____ _____ _____ _____.

2. surprise had a turned when she eighteen she

   She _____ ____ _____ _____ _____ _____ _____ eighteen.

3. food he was house was no because really there in the

   He _____ _____ _____ _____ _____ _____ _____ _____ _____ house.

4. posh very the phone sounded on the

   The _____ _____ _____ _____ _____ _____ phone.

5. and had terrible he to go to leg had a hospital

   He _____ ____ _____ _____ _____ _____ _____ _____ _____ _____ hospital.

Worksheet 5 Answers

Rule 4: Y says the name of 'e' at the end of words

Exercise 2

1. You might have to see a doctor if you get an injury.

2. When you haven't eaten enough food, you can feel really hungry.

3. Sometimes it's really hard to store spellings in your memory.

4. He was a gentleman and she was a lady.

5. When we celebrate something, we can have a party.

Exercise 3

1. Old people can sometimes lose their memory.

2. She had a surprise party when she turned eighteen.

3. He was really hungry because there was no food in the house.

4. The lady sounded very posh on the phone.

5. He had a terrible leg injury and had to go to hospital.

Worksheet 6

Rule 5: Doubling L, S, Z and F after a short vowel sound

l, **s**, **z** and **f** double when coming after a **short vowel sound** at the end of a **syllable** e.g. cuddle, messy, fizzing, huffed. These letters are sometimes called 'flossy' letters.

1. **Read out loud** the following words, using the rule: Doubling 'l', 'z', 'f' and 's' after a short vowel sound at the end of a syllable.

doll

buzz

fluff

mess

trolley

fizzing

different

guess

windmill

2. **Spell** the following words using Rule 5 and the clues and pictures to help you.

If the learner is struggling to find the word, use 'hangman' to help you get the answer.

1. You can use your nose to smell and to _____.

2. A slithering snake can stick out its tongue and _____.

3. You find them on the beach and you can

collect them: _____.

4. When things are untidy, they are_____.

5. If you haven't warmed up your muscles,

they can feel really_____.

3. **Rewrite** the following words into the correct order in the sentence. Add one of the missing **double l, z, f or s words** from activity 2 to complete each sentence.

1. seashore the sea on

   Sea _____ _____ _____ seashore.

2. it hurts I with a woke up neck and

   I _____ _____ _____ ____ _____ _____ _____ _____ hurts.

3. cold you when have you a

   You _____ _____ _____ _____ _____ cold.

4. it room is so tidy your

   Tidy _____ _____! _____ _____ _____ _____!

5. Cat did at me that just

   Did _____ _____ _____ _____ _____ me?

Worksheet 6 Answers

Rule 5: Doubling L, S, Z and F after a short vowel sound

Exercise 2

1. You can use your nose to smell and to sniff.

2. A slithering snake can stick out its tongue and hiss.

3. You find them on the beach and you can collect them: shells

4. When things are untidy, they are messy.

5. If you haven't warmed up your muscles, they can feel really stiff.

Exercise 3

1. Sea shells on the seashore.

2. I woke up with a stiff neck and it hurts.

3. You sniff when you have a cold.

4. Tidy your room! It is so messy!

5. Did that cat just hiss at me?

Worksheet 7

Rule 6: C before K after a short vowel sound

c comes before **k** after a **short vowel sound** at the end of a **syllable**.
e.g. pick or picking

1. **Read out loud** the following words using the rule: 'c' comes before 'k' after a short vowel sound (at the end of a syllable).

Words with syllables ending in 'ck' after a short vowel sound

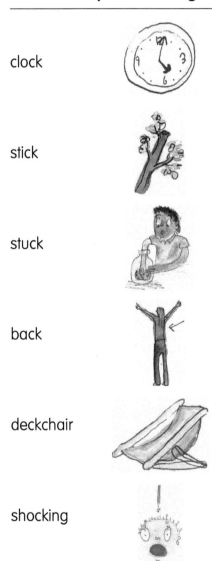

clock

stick

stuck

back

deckchair

shocking

haystack

blackboard

freckles

2. **Spell** the following words using the Rule 6 and the clues and pictures to help you.

If the learner is struggling to find the word, use 'hangman' to help you get the answer.

1. **He drove around in his large** _____.

2. **A witch's cat tends to be this colour:**_____.

3. **Try not to do this with your nose, it's disgusting!** _____.

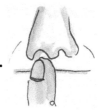

4. **Your head is attached to your:**_____.

5. **You put this on your foot to keep it warm:**_____.

3. **Rewrite** the following words into the correct order in the sentence. Add one of the missing **'ck' words** from activity 2 to complete each sentence.

1. was night's hair sky as the as her

   Her _____ _____ ____ _____ ____ ___ _____ sky.

2. to wildflowers try meadow not the in the

   Try _____ ____ _____ ____ _____ ____ _____ meadow.

3. warm foot your keeps a

   A _____ _____ _____ _____ warm.

4. hurt he whilst rugby his playing

   He _____ _____ _____ _____ _____ rugby.

5. pick-up a he green drove

   He _____ _____ _____ _____-_____ _____ .

Worksheet 7 Answers

Rule 6: C before K after a short vowel sound

Exercise 2

1. He drove around in his large truck.

2. A witch's cat tends to be this colour: black

3. Try not to do this with your nose, it's disgusting! pick

4. Your head is attached to your neck.

5. You put this on your foot to keep it warm: sock

Exercise 3

1. Her hair was as black as the night's sky.

2. Try not to pick the wildflowers in the meadow.

3. A sock keeps your foot warm.

4. He hurt his neck whilst playing rugby.

5. He drove a green pick-up truck.

Worksheet 8

Rule 7: T, C and H after a short vowel sound

t, **c** and **h** can go together after a **short vowel sound** at the end of a **syllable**.
e.g. catch or catching

1. **Read out loud** the following words:

Words ending in 'tch' that follow a single, short vowel sound:

switch

stretch

stitch

thatch

sketch

snatch

patch

fetch

butterscotch

2. **Spell** the following **'tch' words** using Rule 7 and the clues and pictures to help you.

If the learner is struggling to find the word, use 'hangman' to help you get the answer.

1. You can light a fire with a _____.

2. The broomstick and cat belong to the _____.

3. A pet rabbit tends to live in a _____.

4. Using a ball, we need to learn how to throw

and _____.

5. When a chick is ready, we see an egg begin

to _____.

3. **Rewrite** the following words into the correct order in the sentence. Add one of the missing **'tch' word**s from activity 2 to complete each sentence.

1. cat a has black nasty a

   A _____ _____ _____ _____ _____ cat.

2. see the egg did you

   Did _____ _____ _____ _____ _____?

3. left the rabbit open who

   Who _____ _____ _____ _____ open?

4. finger sore I to hard find it with my

   I _____ _____ _____ _____ _____ _____ _____ _____ finger.

5. going to I see am team play in a my

   I _____ _____ _____ _____ _____ _____ _____ _____ _____ _____.

Worksheet 8 Answers

Rule 7: T, C and H after a short vowel sound

Exercise 2

1. You can light a fire with a match.

2. The broomstick and cat belong to the witch.

3. A pet rabbit tends to live in a hutch.

4. With a ball, we need to learn how to throw and catch.

5. When a chick is ready, we see an egg begin to hatch.

Exercise 3

1. A nasty witch has a black cat.

2. Did you see the egg hatch?

3. Who left the rabbit hutch open?

4. I find it hard to catch with my sore finger.

5. I am going to see my team play in a match.

Worksheet 9

Rule 8: S before H after a short vowel sound

s comes before **h** after a **short vowel sound** at the end of a **syllable**.
e.g. push or pushing

1. **Read out loud** the following words:

Words ending in /sh/ that follow a single, short vowel sound

---

rash

fish

lush

push

fresh

smash

crush

wish

cherish

finish

2. **Spell** the following **'sh' words** using Rule 8 and the clues and pictures to help you:

If the learner is struggling to find the word, use 'hangman' to help you get the answer.

1. **This pastry can also be the name of someone**

   from Denmark: _____.

2. **This golden pond creature swims round and**

   round in a bowl: _____.

3. **Another name for nail varnish is nail** _____.

4. **To paint your nails or walls, you use a** _____.

5. People who are fancy, high-class or elegant can be _____.

3. **Rewrite** the following words into the correct order in the sentence. Add one of the missing '**sh' words** from activity 2 to complete each sentence.

1. **Out the Starboard acronym for Port is Home**

   The _____ _____ _____ _____ _____, _____ _____.

2. **of memory some say seconds 3 the a is only long**

   Some _____ _____ _____ ____ ____ _____ ____ _____ ____ _____
   long.

3. **Swedish was speaking he or**

   Was _____ _____ _____ _____ **Swedish?**

4. **It is your messy please hair, very**

   Please _____ _____ _____, _____ _____ _____ **messy.**

5. **very If you shiny silver, it makes it**

   If _____ _____ _____, _____ _____ _____ _____ **shiny.**

Worksheet 9 Answers

Rule 8: S before H after a short vowel sound

Exercise 2

1. This pastry can also be the name of someone from Denmark – Danish pastry

2. This golden pond creature swims round and round in a bowl: goldfish

3. Another name for nail varnish is nail: polish

4. To paint your nails or walls, you use a: brush

5. People who are fancy, high-class or elegant – can be posh.

Exercise 3

1. The acronym POSH is for Port Out, Starboard Home.

2. Some say the memory of a goldfish is only 3 seconds long.

3. Was he speaking Danish or Swedish?

4. Please brush your hair, it is very messy.

5. If you polish silver, it makes it very shiny.

Worksheet 10

Rule 9: S makes plurals and helps verbs agree

s is added to the end of most words to make **plurals** or **verb agreements**
e.g. many cats (plural) or she eats (verb agreement)

1. **Read out loud** the following words:

NB: Have fun discussing how these could be used in different contexts e.g. He loves reading books but she always books the tickets for their holidays.

Plural nouns ending in 's'

dogs *(plural noun)*

books *(plural noun and verb)*

chairs *(plural noun and verb)*

seas *(plural noun)*

mountains *(plural noun)*

rivers *(plural noun)*

fields *(plural noun)*

flowers *(plural noun and verb)*

monkeys *(plural noun)*

holidays *(plural noun and verb)*

2. **Spell** the following plural **'s' word** endings using Rule 9 and the clues and pictures to help you:

If the learner is struggling to find the word, use 'hangman' to help you get the answer.

1. Before you write with ink pens you write with _____.

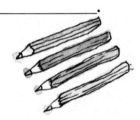

2. People have to get driving licenses so that they

can drive these: _____.

3. Most of these can fly with wings and some

can sing: _____.

4. You need these to lock and unlock:_____.

**5. They look like horses and make an
'ee-ore' sound: _____.**

3. **Rewrite** the following words into the correct order in the sentence. Add one of the missing **'s' word** endings from activity 2 to complete each sentence.

1. **locked she house lost was her and out**

   She _____ _____ _____ _____ _____ _____ _____ **out.**

2. **beaches ride children on some**

   Children _____ _____ _____ _____ **beaches.**

3. **hours he used sharpening to spend**

   He _____ _____ _____ _____ _____ _____.

4. **I morning listening love to in the singing the**

   I _____ _____ ____ ____ _____ _____ ____ ____ **morning.**

5. **racetrack you a can on race**

   You _____ _____ _____ _____ _____ **racetrack.**

Worksheet 10 Answers

Rule 9: S makes plurals and helps verbs agree

Exercise 2

1. Before you write with ink pens you write with pencils.

2. People have to get driving licenses so that they can drive these: cars

3. Most of these can fly with wings and some can sing: birds

4. You need these to lock and unlock: keys

5. They look like horses and make an 'ee-ore' sound: donkeys

Exercise 3

1. She lost her house keys and was locked out.

2. Children ride donkeys on some beaches.

3. He used to spend hours sharpening pencils.

4. I love listening to the birds singing in the morning.

5. Some people drive cars but you can also collect them.

Worksheet 11

> ## Rule 10: E and S make plurals and help verbs agree (after hissing sounds)
>
> **e** and **s** are added to words ending with hissing sounds like **ch**, **s**, **sh**, **x** and **z** when becoming **plurals** or **verb agreements** e.g. many churches or she dashes

1. **Read out loud** the following words:

NB: Have fun discussing how these could be used in different contexts e.g. The ballerina bunches up her hair and she is often given bunches of flowers after a performance.

Plural nouns and verb agreements ending in 'es':

Foxes *(plural noun)*

Bunches *(plural noun and verb)*

Houses *(plural noun)*

Bushes *(plural noun)*

Buzzes *(verb)*

Hisses *(verb)*

Reaches *(verb)*

Fixes *(verb)*

Kisses *(plural noun and verb)*

Finishes *(verb)*

2. **Spell** the following **'es' words** using Rule 10 and the clues and pictures to help you.

If the learner is struggling to find the word, use 'hangman' to help you get the answer.

1. **People can pray inside these:** _____.

2. **If you shake a soda drink it:** _____.

3. **If a car bumps into another car**

   it: _____.

4. **If you add ingredients together, the mixture:** _____.

5. When a snake makes a sound it: _____.

3. **Rewrite** the following words into the correct order in the sentence. Add one of the missing **'es' words** from activity 2 to complete each sentence.

1. bike his are broken so brakes he often his

   His _____ _____ _____ _____ _____ _____ _____ _____ bike.

2. pray regularly in Christians

   Christians _____ _____ _____ _____.

3. mouth in Coca Cola your

   Coca Cola _____ _____ _____ mouth.

4. its a predators python at

   A _____ _____ _____ _____ predators.

5. a well with a Labradoodle Labrador a Poodle to make

   A _____ _____ _____ _____ ___ _____ ____ _____ a Labradoodle.

Worksheet 11 Answers

Rule 10 E and S make plurals and help verbs agree (after hissing sounds)

Exercise 2

1. People can pray inside these: churches

2. If you shake a soda drink it: fizzes.

3. If a car bumps into another car it: crashes.

4. If you add ingredients together, the mixture: mixes.

5. When a snake makes a sound, it hisses.

Exercise 3

1. His brakes are broken so he often crashes his bike.

2. Christians regularly pray in churches.

3. Coca Cola fizzes in your mouth.

4. A python hisses at its predators.

5. A Poodle mixes well with a Labrador to make a Labradoodle.

Worksheet 12

> ## Rule 11: F is replaced by VES when making plurals
>
> **f** is replaced by **ves** at the end of words when making **plural nouns**.
> e.g. leaf/leaves

NB: Some words ending in 'f' have two forms of the plural:

- dwarf – dwarfs or dwarves
- hoof – hoofs or hooves
- scarf – scarfs or scarves
- staff – staffs or staves
- wharf – wharfs or wharves

1. **Read out loud** the following words:

Words ending in 'ves'

---

shelf – shelves

calf – calves

wife – wives

half – halves

Loaf – loaves

knife – knives

self – selves

wolf – wolves

thief – thieves

elf – elves

2. **Spell** the following **'ves' words** using Rule 11 and the clues and pictures to help you:

If the learner is struggling to find the word, use 'hangman' to help you get the answer.

1. These dangerous animals are found in the wilds of

places like Alaska and Siberia: _____.

2. When people take 'selfies', they take pictures

of _____.

3. Henry the VIII had six of

these: _____.

4. A cat is supposed to have nine of these: _____.

5. Small tools with sharp blades folding into the handle:
_____.

3. **Rewrite** the following words into the correct order in the sentence. Add one of the missing **'ves' words** from activity 2 to complete each sentence.

1. when shocked they they were saw on film

When _____ _____ _____ _____ _____, _____ _____ shocked!

2. have fold handle into gadgets that the

_____ _____ _____ _____ _____ _____ _____ handle.

3. allowed Mormon many men are

Mormon _____ _____ _____ _____ _____.

4. are these the our days of

These _____ _____ _____ _____ _____ _____.

5. hunters hunt that in are fierce packs

_____ _____ _____ _____ _____ _____ _____ packs.

Worksheet 12 Answers

Rule 11: F is replaced by VES when making plurals

Exercise 2

1. These dangerous animals are found in the wilds of places like Alaska and Siberia: wolves

2. When people take 'selfies', they take pictures of: themselves

3. Henry the VIII had six of these: wives

4. A cat is supposed to have 9 of these: lives

5. Small tools with sharp blades folding into the handle: penknives

Exercise 3

1. When they saw themselves on film, they were shocked!

2. Penknives have gadgets that fold into the handle.

3. Mormon men are allowed many wives.

4. These are the days of our lives.

5. Wolves are fierce hunters that hunt in packs.

Worksheet 13

> ## Rule 12: I, E and S make plurals
>
> **y** is replaced with '**ies**' at the end of words when making them **plural** and helps verbs agree with **subjects**. e.g. Halloween parties or she parties all the time!

1. Read out loud the following words:

NB: Have fun discussing how these could be used in different contexts e.g. He tries really hard to score tries in rugby.

Plural nouns and verb agreements ending in 'ies':

curry – curries *(plural noun and verb agreement)*

hurry – hurries *(verb agreement)*

berry – berries *(plural noun)*

bury – buries *(verb agreement)*

bunny – bunnies *(plural noun)*

carry – carries *(verb agreement)*

marry – marries *(verb agreement)*

bully – bullies *(plural noun and verb agreement)*

buggy – buggies *(plural noun)*

worry – worries *(verb agreement)*

2. **Spell** the following **'ies' words** using Rule 12 and the clues and pictures to help you:

If the learner is struggling to find the word, use 'hangman' to help you get the answer.

   1. **These are also known as trucks:** _____.

   2. **These are often eaten in the summer as sweet, ice** _____.

   3. **Young children, especially girls, love to play with these:** _____.

   4. **He can try to score many of these in rugby:** _____.

5. If you fry potatoes in France you can get these: _____ _____.

3. **Rewrite** the following words into the correct order in the sentence. Add one of the missing **'ies' ending words** from activity 2 to complete the sentence.

1. **eating I like ketchup with**

   I _____ _____ _____ _____ _____ ketchup.

2. **your you lick lovely tongue with**

   You _____ _____ _____ _____ _____ tongue.

3. **in you score a game of rugby**

   In _____ _____ _____ _____ _____ _____ _____.

4. **to another transport from goods one place**

   _____ _____ _____ _____ _____ _____ _____ another.

5. **has many toys she so and**

   she _____ _____ _____ _____ _____ _____!

Worksheet 13 Answers

Rule 12: I, E and S make plurals

Exercise 2

1. These are also known as trucks: lorries

2. These are often eaten in the summer as sweet, ice lollies

3. Young children, especially girls, love to play with these: dollies

4. He can try to score many of these in rugby: tries

5. If you fry potatoes in France you can get these: French fries

Exercise 3

1. I like eating French fries with ketchup.

2. You lick lovely lollies with your tongue.

3. In a game of rugby, you score tries.

4. Lorries transport goods from one place to another.

5. She has so many toys and dollies!

Worksheet 14

Rule 13: O can end some words

The letter name 'o' can end words like hello, potato and halo.

1. **Read out loud** the following words:

Words ending in the letter name for 'o':

no

go

banjo

halo

radio

potato

gazebo

memento

tomato

buffalo

2. **Spell** the following **'o' words** using Rule 13 and the clues and pictures to help you:

If the learner is struggling to find the word, use 'hangman' to help you get the answer.

1. **A greeting you say to welcome someone: "_____".**

2. **Someone who can save the world (usually wearing**

   a cape): _____.

3. **A sport of self-defence or fighting: _____.**

4. **The number or digit that means 'nothing': _____.**

5. **A delicious fruit often found in India: _____.**

3. **Rewrite** the following words into the correct order in the sentence. Add one of the missing words with the **'o' ending** from activity 2 to complete each sentence.

1. or a is a villain Batman

   Is _____ _____ _____ _____ _____ _____-_____?

2. the number a very digit is important

   The _____ '_____' _____ _____ _____ _____ digit.

3. I 'goodbye' prefer than to to say say

   I _____ _____ _____ '_____' _____ _____ _____ 'goodbye'.

4. ability in colour the of your belt your shows

   In _____, _____ _____ ____ _____ _____ _____ _____ ability.

5. and juicy a is a fruit delicious

   A _____ _____ _____ _____ _____ _____ fruit.

Worksheet 14 Answers

Rule 13: O can end some words

Exercise 2

1. A greeting you say to welcome someone: "hello"

2. Someone who can save the world (usually wearing a cape): super-hero

3. A sport of self-defence or fighting: judo

4. The number or digit that means 'nothing': zero

5. A delicious fruit often found in the Caribbean: mango

Exercise 3

1. Is Batman a villain or a super-hero?

2. The number 'zero' is a very important digit.

3. I prefer to say 'hello' than to say 'goodbye'.

4. In Judo, the colour of your belt shows your ability.

5. A mango is a delicious and juicy fruit.

Worksheet 15

Rule 14: A can introduce words

The letter name 'a' can be used as a word to introduce most **nouns**. It is a **determiner** and helps us to know what is coming next. e.g. a beautiful dress

Rule 15: A and N join together to introduce nouns beginning with vowel sounds

a and **n** join together as '**an**' to introduce **nouns** beginning with **vowel** sounds. '**an**' is a **determiner** and helps us to know what is coming next. e.g. an orange or an elegant lady

NB: The **nouns** may be described by an **adjective** so the **determiner** will match the **adjective** e.g. a smelly sock or an old man

(*Reminder: A **determiner** tells us what noun or noun group is coming next (it might include an adjective) e.g. an awkward situation or a gorgeous gorilla.*)

1. **Read out loud** the following words:

_____

The determiners 'a' and 'an':

_____

An apple

A person

An igloo

A table

An egg

A fork

An orange

A car

An umbrella

A pair of shoes

2. **Spell** the following **'a'** or **'an' determiners** using Rules 14 and 15 and the clues and pictures to help you:

1. __ **beautiful baby boy.**

2. __ elephant is squirting water.

3. __ pair of smelly socks.

4. __ awesome computer game.

5. __ flock of sheep.

3. **Rewrite** the following words into the correct order in the sentence. Add the missing 'a' or 'an' determiners to complete the sentence.

1. pack journey of essential for long cards is

___ _____ ___ _____ ___ _____ ____ ___ _____ _____!

2. lemon orange is than sweeter

____ _____ _____ ___ _____ _____ _____ _____.

3. want when grow person up, you to be independent you

When ___ _____ __, ___ _____ __ __ _____ _____ _____.

4. human be person can extraordinary

____ _____ _____ _____ ____ _____ _____.

5. or Inuit can igloo Eskimo live in

___ _____ (__ ___ _____) _____ _____ ____ ___ _____.

Worksheet 15 Answers

Rule 14: A can introduce words

Rule 15: A and N join together to introduce nouns beginning with vowel sounds

Exercise

1. A beautiful baby boy.

2. An elephant is squirting water.

3. A pair of smelly socks.

4. An awesome computer game.

5. A flock of sheep.

Exercise

1. A pack of cards is essential for a long journey.

2. An orange is sweeter than a lemon.

3. When you grow up, you want to be an independent person.

4. A human can be an extraordinary person.

5. An Eskimo (or an Inuit) can live in an igloo.

Worksheet 16

Rule 16: 'I' is a word on its own

i can be a word on its own (**subject pronoun**), but it must always be written with a capital **I**. e.g. I am tired

'**I**' on its own is a **subject pronoun**. Do you remember what '**subject**' means? *It is the person or thing doing the action e.g. I am throwing a ball to the dog. (It is 'me' doing the throwing so I am the subject).*

A **pronoun** is a word that replaces the **noun** in the sentence – it makes it shorter and easier to write or say. So instead of me, 'Georgie' throwing the ball, I have replaced Georgie with '**I**'. *I am throwing a ball to the dog.*

'**I**' is the only subject pronoun that is one letter standing on its own. Other subject pronouns are:

- You

- He

- She

- It

- They

Complete the following sentences to make sure you feel happy using the pronoun 'I'. Replace the blank name with 'I' and then follow it with a correct **verb agreement**. e.g. I like sausages and mash.

N.B. Answers will vary depending on the learner's likes and dislikes.

a) __ _____ playing computer games.

b) __ _____ school!

c) __ _____ spelling and writing.

d) __ _____ maths.

e) __ _____ after school activities, __ especially enjoy doing _____.

Now write one sentence about school, using the pronoun 'I' at least twice.

_____

_____

_____

Worksheet 17

Rule 17: I before E except after C

i comes before **e** except after **c** when we hear the **e**'s name
e.g. receive and deceive

NB: In most exceptions to this rule, you hear 'a's name e.g. neighbour or weigh

1. **Read out loud** the following words:

Words spelt with i before e except after c

chief

field

grief

piece

priest

pierce

fierce

achieve

mischief

diesel

2. **Spell** the following **'i' before 'e' words** using Rule 17 and the clues and pictures to help you.

   If the learner is struggling to find the word, use 'hangman' to help you get the answer.

   1. A person who steals is also known as a: _____.

   2. When you believe in something you have: _____.

   3. This case is used by business men and

   women: _____.

4. Taking care of health and keeping clean: _____.

5. A daughter of a person's brother or sister: _____.

3. **Rewrite** the following words into the correct order in the sentence. Add in the missing **'i' before 'e' words** from activity 2 to complete the sentence.

1. office his he left at the

   He _____ _____ _____ _____ _____ office!

2. his armpits not is good, his smell

   His _____ _____ _____ _____, _____ _____ smell!

3. have I great do well that you will

   I _____ _____ _____ _____ _____ _____ _____ well.

4. has my hey stop he bag that

   Hey! _____ _____ _____! _____ _____ _____ _____!

5. favourite uncle am John says I his

   Uncle _____ _____ _____ _____ _____ _____ _____.

Don't forget that this rule doesn't apply to words making /ee/ sounds where 'e' and 'i' follow 'c'. Here are some examples:

- receive

- deceive

- receipt

- perceive

a) Read this out loud:

   I **conceived** this (a plan):

   "I **perceive** your **deceit** from the **receipt** I saw, stuck on the **ceiling**.

   What **conceit** you have!"

b) Complete this sentence with the missing 'i' before 'e' except after 'c' rule:

   If you look up from your bed, you will be staring at the _____.

Worksheet 17 Answers

Rule 17: I before E except after C

Exercise 2

1. A person who steals is also known as a: thief

2. When you believe in something you have: belief

3. This case is used by business men and women: briefcase

4. Taking care of health and keeping clean: hygiene

5. A daughter of a person's brother or sister: niece

Exercise 3

1. He left his briefcase at the office!

2. His hygiene is not good, his armpits smell!

3. I have great belief that you will do well.

4. Hey! Stop that thief! He has my bag!

5. Uncle John says I am his favourite niece.

Extra exercises

a) I conceived this (a plan):

   "I perceive your deceit from the receipt I saw, stuck on the ceiling.

   What conceit you have!"

b) If you look up from your bed, you will be staring at the ceiling.

Worksheet 18

Rule 18: Q before U

Where there is a **q**, it is always followed by **u**. e.g. quiet or square

1. **Read out loud** the following words:

'qu' words:

queen

quiet

quid

quad-bike

quake

quack

quiff

quiche

quick

quiz

2. **Spell** the following **'qu' words** using Rule 18 and the clues and pictures to help you.

If the learner is struggling to find the word, use 'hangman' to help you get the answer.

1. This is one fourth: _____.

2. This is a four cornered courtyard: _____.

3. This is an adverb and a synonym **for 'hurry':** _____.

4. This is an adverb and an antonym **for**

'loudly': _____.

5. When someone or something is unique or

different: _____.

3. **Rewrite** the following words into the correct order in the sentence. Add in the missing **'qu' words** from activity 2 to complete the sentence:

1. race you need run to to win a

   You _____ _____ _____ _____ _____ _____ _____ race.

2. the in the together pupils gathered

   The _____ _____ _____ _____ _____ _____.

3. is really Sam but him I like

   Sam _____ _____ _____ _____ _____ _____ him.

4. she baby's when tip-toed she cot passed the

   She _____-_____ _____ _____ _____ _____

   _____ _____ cot.

5. afternoon it is a to four the in

   It _____ _____ _____ _____ _____ _____ _____ afternoon.

Worksheet 18 Answers

Rule 18: Q before U

Exercise 2

1. This is one fourth: quarter

2. This is a four cornered courtyard: quad/quadrangle

3. This is an adverb and a synonym for 'hurry': quickly

4. This is an adverb and an antonym for 'loudly': quietly

5. When someone or something is unique or different: quirky

Exercise 3

1. You need to run quickly to win the race.

2. The pupils gathered together in the quad.

3. Sam is really quirky but I like him.

4. She tip-toed quietly when she passed the baby's cot.

5. It is a quarter to four in the afternoon.

Worksheet 19

Rule 19: W can change vowel sounds

w can change vowel sounds that follow in words (mainly /**o**/ and /**a**/).
e.g. was or work

N.B: This rule affects 'o' and 'a' the most.

Irregular High frequency words: was, want, wasn't are good examples to discuss.

1. **Read out loud** the following words:

'w' + vowel sound words:

war (/or/)

wand (/o/)

wallet (/o/)

world (/ur/)

water (/or/)

work (/ur/)

word (/ur/)

waffle (/o/)

swamp (/o/)

swat (/o/)

2. **Spell** the following **'w' words** using Rule 19 and the clues and pictures to help you.

If the learner is struggling to find the word, use 'hangman' to help you get the answer.

1. **This looks like a bee and stings:** _____.

2. **Another word to 'exchange' with someone:** _____.

3. **A growth on one's skin. Witches often have them:** _____.

4. A synonym for 'thinking': _____.

5. A word for someone who is looking around

(like a tourist): _____.

3. **Rewrite** the following words into the correct order in the sentence. Adding in the missing **'w' words** from activity 2 to complete the sentence.

1. this exam I am if I pass will

I _____ _____ _____ _____ _____ _____ _____ _____?

2. by a I been stung have

I _____ _____ _____ _____ _____ _____!

3. your will stickers with you one of me

Will _____ _____ _____ _____ _____ _____ _____

_____?

4. trying to find he is around car his

He _____ _____ _____ _____ _____ _____ _____

_____.

5. has she on her nose a horrible

She _____ _____ _____ _____ _____ _____ _____.

Worksheet 19 Answers

Rule 19: W can change vowel sounds

Exercise 2

1. This looks like a bee and stings: wasp

2. Another word to 'exchange' with someone: swap

3. A growth on one's skin. Witches often have them: wart/s

4. A synonym for 'thinking': wondering

5. A word for someone who is looking around (like a tourist): wandering

Exercise 3

1. I am wondering if I will pass this exam?

2. I have been stung by a wasp.

3. Will you swap one of your stickers with me?

4. He is wandering around trying to find his car.

5. She has a horrible wart on her nose.

Worksheet 20

Rule 20: T can change irregular verbs into the past

t can change **irregular verbs** to put them into the past tense (instead of adding the suffix -ed) e.g. slept and felt

Remember that irregular verbs tend not to follow rules! They like to be spelt differently. Some of the following words can also be spelt with –ed at the end e.g. spelt/spelled.

1. **Read out loud** the following words:

Irregular past tense verbs ending in 't':

---

slept

wept

crept

bent

burnt

learnt

felt

dreamt

leapt

spoilt

2. **Spell** the following **irregular 't' verbs** using Rule 20 and the clues and pictures to help you.

If the learner is struggling to find the word, use 'hangman' to help you get the answer.

1. **The pheasant was _____ by the poacher.**

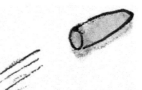

2. **He _____ the house all by himself.**

3. **Guy Fawkes was _____ on a bonfire.**

4. She _____ him some money but he didn't pay her back.

5. He _____ all of his pocket money on a computer game.

3. Choose (from above) **five** irregular verbs ending in **'t'**, to write five sentences in the past tense:

1.

_____

_____

2.

_____

_____

3.

_____

_____

4.

_____

_____

5.

_____

_____

Worksheet 20 Answers

Rule 20: T can change irregular verbs into the past

Exercise 2

1. The pheasant was shot by the poacher.

2. He built the house all by himself.

3. Guy Fawkes was burnt on a bonfire.

4. She lent him some money but he didn't pay her back.

5. He spent all of his pocket money on a computer game.

Exercise 3

Answers may vary.

Worksheet 21

> ## Rule 21: Copycat C
>
> **c** can copy the sounds for **s** (soft c) and **k** (hard c)
> e.g. city, cent, cycle or cat, cup, cod

Soft 'c' – is followed by 'y', 'i' or 'e'

Hard 'c' – is followed by 'a', 'o' or 'u'

N.B: 'g' can also be soft or hard, following the same rules.

1. **Read out loud** the following words:

Are these hard or soft 'c'?		Are these hard or soft 'g'?	
city		gate	
cat		gun	
cute		gel	
cent		gym	
bicycle		gold	

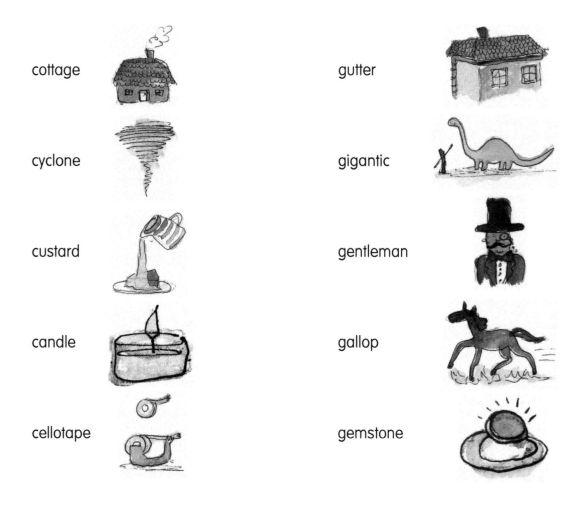

cottage

cyclone

custard

candle

cellotape

gutter

gigantic

gentleman

gallop

gemstone

2. **Spell** the following **'soft c', 'soft g', 'hard c', 'hard g' words** using Rule 21 and the clues and pictures to help you.

If the learner is struggling to find the word, use 'hangman' to help you get the answer.

1. 100 years or a hundred runs in cricket is called a _____.

2. You pull these to block light coming through a

window: _____.

3. It is an orange vegetable and donkeys love to eat

them: _____.

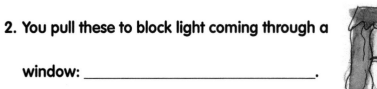

4. A shape that goes round and round … : _____.

5. Like a bike but it has a motor to make it go

faster: _____.

6. Someone/thing protecting you from harm or keeping you

secure: _____.

7. A lively animal that gives good milk and makes a bleating

noise: _____.

8. A very large being, often found in fairytales: _____.

9. A thick, clear, sometimes sticky substance: _____.

10. Where grass and flowers grow outside a

    house: _____.

11. A person coming from Egypt is called

    an _____.

3. **Write** two sentences. One should include **'soft and hard c' words** and the other should include **'soft and hard g' words**.

    1.

    _____

    _____

    2.

    _____

    _____

Worksheet 21 Answers

Rule 21: Copycat C

'g' can also be soft or hard, following the same rules.

Exercise 1

Are these hard or soft 'c'?	Are these hard or soft 'g'
city – soft 'c'	gate – hard 'g'
cat – hard 'c'	gun – hard 'g'
cute – hard 'c'	gel – soft 'g'
cent – soft 'c'	gym – soft 'g'
bicycle – soft 'c'	gold – hard 'g'
cottage – hard 'c'	gutter – hard 'g'
cyclone – soft 'c'	gigantic - soft 'g' followed by hard 'g'
custard – hard 'c'	gentleman soft 'g'
candle – hard 'c'	gallop hard 'g'
cellotape – soft 'c'	gemstone soft 'g'

Exercise 2

1. 100 years or one hundred runs in cricket is called: century

2. You pull these to block light coming through a window: curtains

3. It is an orange vegetable and donkeys love to eat them: carrot

4. A shape that goes round and round: circle

5. Like a bike but it has a motor to make it go faster: motorcycle

6. Someone/thing protecting you from harm or keeping you secure: guard

7. A lively animal that gives good milk and makes a bleating noise: goat

8. A very large being, often found in fairy tales: giant

9. A thick, clear, sometimes sticky substance: gel

10. Where grass and flowers grow outside a house: garden

11. A person coming from Egypt is called an: Egyptian

Exercise 3

1. and 2. Answers may vary.

Worksheet 22

Rule 22: Y's sound comes at the beginning of words

y's **sound** can only be heard at the beginning of words. e.g. yum and yellow

1. **Read out loud** the following words:

Words starting with /y/:

yak

yolk

yes

yellow

yogurt

yoga

yacht

yawn

yum

you

2. **Spell** the following words starting with **/y/** using Rule 22 and the clues and pictures to help you:

If the learner is struggling to find the word, use 'hangman' to help you get the answer.

1. A synonym for 'shout': _____.

2. An expression showing distaste!: _____.

3. You're the opposite of old: _____.

4. A product helping bread to rise: _____.

5. Young people are also known as: _____.

3. **Rewrite** the following words into the correct order in the sentence. Add in the missing **'y' word** from activity 2 to complete the sentence.

1. **should the wise listen to the**

   The _____ _____ _____ _____ _____ wise.

2. **need to you for help**

   You _____ _____ _____ _____ help!

3. **the of environment care about the today**

   The _____ _____ _____ _____ _____ _____ environment.

4. **disgusting that is**

   _____! _____ _____ disgusting!

5. **is flatbread without usually made**

   Flatbread _____ _____ _____ _____ _____.

Worksheet 22 Answers

Rule 22: Y's sound comes at the beginning of words

Exercise 2

1. A synonym for 'shout': yell/yelp

2. An expression showing distaste! Yuck!

3. You're the opposite of old: young

4. A product helping bread to rise: yeast

5. Young people are also known as: youth

Exercise 3

1. The young should listen to the wise.

2. You need to yell for help!

3. The Youth of today care about the environment.

4. Yuck! That is disgusting!

5. Flatbread is usually made without yeast.

Glossary

Adjective This helps to describe the **noun** e.g. the beautiful (adjective) baby (noun)

Adverb This helps to describe the **verb** e.g. he was crying (verb) loudly (adverb)

Alliteration When closely connected words start with the same letter or sound

Antonym A word with the opposite meaning of another word e.g. loud and quiet

Consonant digraphs Two consonants making one sound e.g. ch, ph, ck, sh

Consonants All the individual letters of the alphabet apart from vowels

Decoding The process of applying word attack strategies to work out how to read an unknown word. This often involves building or blending sounds together to help recognise the unknown word e.g. c-a-t is 'cat'

Determiner This tells us what noun or noun group is coming next (it might include an adjective) e.g. a or an

Digraphs Two letters together making one sound e.g. ai or th

Encoding The process of applying known patterns in spellings to help spell unknown words

Graphemes The written representation of a phoneme or a unit of sound e.g. 'a' or 'k'

Irregular verb A verb in which the past tense is not made by adding an -ed ending (like regular verb endings) e.g. 'sell' is 'sold' in the past tense

Neurodiversity A range of differences in the functioning and behaviour of an individual brain

Noun A person, place or thing e.g. man, home, dog

Object The part of the sentence that is having something done to it e.g. the cat sat on the *mat*

Orthography The learning of spelling and how letters combine to represent sounds and form words

Phonemes Units of individual sounds e.g. /a/, /oi/, /ch/, /igh/, /t/

Phonemic awareness The ability to hear, identify and manipulate phonemes

Phonics This is a method for teaching reading and writing of the English language by developing learners' phonemic awareness: the ability to hear, identify, and manipulate phonemes. This is needed to then teach the relationship between these sounds and the spelling patterns that represent them.

Phonological awareness The ability to hear, identify and manipulate rhyme, syllables and phonemes

Phonology The organisation system of sounds in language

Processing (memory) This is one stage of helping the memory. In simple terms, our brains receive information and the processing is how long it takes to receive that information – do something with it (store it) and then later, retrieve that information in order to show that you have memorised it.

Pronoun A word that replaces the noun in the sentence – it makes it shorter and easier to write or say; 'I' on its own is a **subject pronoun**

Plural noun A plural noun is a word that indicates that there is more than one person, animal place, thing, or idea

Rhyme Corresponding sounds, usually at the end of words that sound the same e.g. ill/thrill; these do not have to be spelt with the same pattern but just need to sound the same e.g. hair/bear

Rimes Usually the written representation of rhyming words, belonging to the same word family e.g. beach, sea, tea, cream, read etc

Schwa In simple terms, this is an 'uh' sound at the end of a single sound. Examples of this would be 'buh' for the letter 'b'. If said with a schwa, the word 'but' could end up sounding like 'buh – uh – tuh' or 'butter'. It's very important to keep the sounds short.

Subject The part of the sentence that is doing something to an object e.g. the *cat* sat on the mat

Subject verb agreements Subject verb agreement simply means the subject and verb must agree in number. This means both need to be singular or both need to be plural.

Syllable A spoken sound (or beat) containing a vowel sound. You can have a number of different types of syllables but they must all have a vowel sound (including the letter 'y' in words such as: fly, by, my, cry).

Synonym A word with the same meaning as another word e.g. quick and fast

Verb An action word e.g. cry or swim

Vowel digraphs Two vowels making one sound e.g. ai, ee, oi, oa, oo etc. 'If two vowels go walking, the first one does the talking.'

Vowels 5 letters in the alphabet: a, e, i, o, u (y can also make a vowel sound)